From Rags

To

Spiritual Riches

A father's story of his journey from poverty, addiction, and

homelessness to a rich life as a counselor, minister, artist,

author and owner of his company Fibers of Life, LLC.

Johnny L. O'Bryant, Junior

Legal Notes

Author and Publisher Johnny L. O'Bryant, Jr.

From Rags to Spiritual Riches

© 2015 Johnny O'Bryant, Jr.

Library of Congress Cataloging-in-Publication Data

13 ISBN: 978-0-692-44198-5

Manufactured in the United States of America,

at Emprint/Moran Printing, Inc.

Dedication

To my son Johnny III, who allowed me to be

a father, who encouraged me to become great and

pushed me to the limit... I love you son!

My mentor Daryl Cambre who helped me

understand the role of a father in a son's life.

Angela thanks for your forgiveness and

unconditional love and support. It has motivated me to

become a father to our son.

And to all the wonderful people God put in my

life... Especially The Faith Chapel Church of God.

Author's Note

My hope is that you chose to read this book because you know of someone who needs to find a way out of poverty, hopelessness and addiction. As you will discover, I've been there; to hell and back.

It is my strongest desire to let anyone know that recovery is possible and a life of sane and happy usefulness is possible if one is willing to lay aside all old ideals and beliefs and embrace a new conception.

Today, working in the field of addiction, studying to become a minister and sponsoring guys in the fellowship of Alcoholics Anonymous have given me the necessary information to help others.

Some of us didn't ask for the hand that life dealt us. Nothing changed until I came to the realization that enough was enough. Everything I've written here is true to the best of my memory. I wanted to set down 8 in writing the story of the love of my son, who was fatherless for a while, and of me, his father, who was always a fatherless son.

For the purpose of anonymity and the confidentiality of others, this story does not name names. I'm sure you can draw your own opinion and conclusion.

I've heard it read many times over and know by heart that no matter how far down the scale we have gone, we will see how our experience can benefit others. I cling to the thought that in God's hands, the dark past is the greatest possession we have.

Praise Report from (son)

Johnny O'Bryant III

I started to get to know my father during my time in college.

We shared a lot of good experiences that really helped shape my opinion of him. After each experience, I would always ask myself, For a guy who you heard so many negative things about growing up, why did he seem so amazing to be around?_ I got to know this man more and more as each day went by, and each day he was a joy to be around. No one has more of a powerful and heartfelt story than he. I have witnessed his journey as a recovering alcoholic, fighting his past demons, becoming a father, counselor and most of all a man of GOD. He is a great inspiration to me and many others as he continues to progress and change lives.

LSU Forward: 2011-2014
Milwaukee Bucks 2014- Present

Introduction: Hell on Earth

The screams coming from my mother's mouth are unbearable. They always make me feel sick, and full of fear. My mom begs my dad to stop beating her.

I can hear his ranting and rage as he shouts profanity and obscenities to her. I can also hear the blows as his fist pounds into her body and there is no mistaking the slaps; they have a sound all their own.

I am coiled up in a knot in bed with my siblings (probably five of us). The bed is old, with a metal box spring of wire coils. There is no mattress. On top of the metal box spring are layers of rags packed down in the coils and spread out on top of them. There is always the smell of urine. Someone pisses in bed every night.

Our house is a three-room shotgun shack, nestled in the middle of a cotton field about a hundred feet off the main road. There are several holes in the rusty tin roof and when it rains, out came the cans and buckets to catch the water leaking through. Wood rats the size of small cats scurry through the house all night long. They are looking for food, but they are at the wrong house & my parents rarely ever bring food home. Once I ate toothpaste because that was all there was in the house.

Sometimes we have powdered milk or sugar; we eat those straight out of the bag or box.

I hear the screams again, and they are louder this time. I crawl out of bed and make my way to my parents'_ bedroom door. I ease the door open, and see my dad sitting on top of my mom as he punches her in the face, slapping her head from side to side. I rush in, shouting Get off my mama, get off &, and all I remember after that is flying backward into a wall, seeing lots of little tiny stars, my head spinning and crumbling to the floor in pain and confusion.

Finally my dad gets off my mom; she is not moving. He stumbles to the front door and goes outside, probably to piss and smoke a cigarette. I crawl on my hands and knees to get closer to my mother, and I can hear her moaning. When I get to her she opens one eye. Both her eyes are swollen, and there is blood running out of her mouth. Her bottom lip is split in half and her nose is busted and bleeding as well.

I lie beside my mother for a long time and she finally gathers enough strength to stretch out her arms and give me a hug as she pulls me to her side. We can hear the footsteps of my dad as he starts to come back into the house. My mom whispers for me to get up and go back to bed, and I do.

The only other sound I hear is my dad falling across the bed and after that snoring, loud and gurgling.

This is how it was for us most of the time. I was around five years old. Somehow I had heard of God, although we didn't attend church. I drifted off to sleep, praying to God to please help us.

Life in the Cotton Fields

Picking and chopping cotton by hand was the way of life for most folks in Mound Bayou, my rural town in the Mississippi Delta region. It was a time of celebration when the farmers said the cotton crops were ready to be picked. The only ones who didn't pick were babies in diapers. My earliest memory is waking up on a cotton sack where my mom laid me as she picked cotton; the fuller the sack got, the softer the ride felt, until it was completely full and packed; then

I had to walk behind her. I remember that the cotton stalks were taller than I was. It was always good to get to the end of those rows; I always felt free. I could run around and play for a little while until my mom was ready to go back down the rows again, and she carried four to five rows at a time. Back and forth she went as she picked. She was strong, and she picked like a machine.

When she got a sack full she would go to the trailer where there was a big metal scale. A couple of guys would hoist the big round sack packed full onto the scale, making sure it didn't touch the ground.

My mom always did good, and the guys weighing the cotton always let her know that she had picked the most. I would see my mom smile at the compliment. It made her feel good that she could even beat the men who were picking. My mom averaged two to three hundred pounds a day sometimes. But there were days when she just couldn't go, after a beating from my dad, and she would wait until her face healed up some.

My mom would smile when the sharecropper boss would pay her off; then she would say Let's go boy, got to beat that damn school bus to the house to get your brother and sister.

I'm not sure what my mom did with the money she made. I know she had to have her snuff to dip. She would pull out her bottom lip and pour that snuff into it, and then she would get to spitting out this dark brown spit.

She always kept her bottles of liquor hidden around the house. Most of the time she would leave us at home while she would walk uptown. She would stay gone until late in the night and come back home with our dad, and as soon as they got in the house they would start the arguing and fighting. Usually the fight was over which one of them had been cheating or where is the money from working or picking cotton.

I had an older brother and sister, and two more younger than me; we were the oldest of what would eventually be ten children in our family. I enjoyed playtime with my brothers and sister. When our parents weren't home we would play hide-and-go-seek in the cotton, or run down into the field where the tractors and trucks had made a road through it by driving over the same area until there were just dirt tracks.

We never had store bought toys so we had to come up with ways to play and have fun. We made our own toys. Sometimes we would all fill old car tires and tractor tires with dirt, and then roll them as fast as we could and the dust would fly out, making a big long cloud of dust behind us. An old lawn mower tire nailed to a plank was a homemade toy too; we would push that stick and tire until the wheel flew off. We'd nail it back on and do it over and over.

We were small enough to fit inside the big tractor tires, so we would push each other around, rolling over and over until we were completely dizzy and couldn't stand up. Then we'd get out, laughing and falling down.

I remember the homemade go-cart we made. Somehow we scraped up four tires on the side of the road in a pile of trash. The go-cart had one plank down the middle and two planks across each end so that it looked like a wooden _I_. We nailed a tire to each end of the cross-planks. It was the finest car I had ever seen, and it was time to go riding.

Hey, I said, I'm going first. Who's gonna push me?

I will, I will, said my little brother. My big brother, the family bully, said _That piece of contraption ain't gonna make it three feet down the road. He had a tire full of dirt, waiting to make a dust storm and looking like a dust monkey, covered with dust from head to toe. Off we went, my little sister jumping in to help my little brother push me, the wind in my face, laughter in my throat, and my big brother trying to blind us with dust as he ran alongside us. My big sister had the skinny plank with the wheel nailed on the end of it. All of us running down this dirt road in our flour sack clothes, no underwear on, laughing and having fun.

I couldn't wait to start school. My brother and sister said they had breakfast and lunch every day. They talked about how good the food was, and their talking always made me hungrier than I already was.

Both my parents were chronic alcoholics, and they hardly ever bought any food or clothes. We played outside in the winter barefooted because we never had shoes. All our clothes were either hand-me-downs, rags that other poor families didn't want, but they were either too big or too small. Most of the time our usual one piece of clothing was a flour sack with holes cut out of the top and sides for our heads and arms; it looked like a slip or dress. We didn't wear underwear most of the time.

School was great. I loved it, except we never had pencils or paper. Some days we had to walk, I think because my mom and dad didn't pay the school for us to ride the bus. The walk was about two miles, and I would pick up burnt matchsticks along the way so when I got to school I would have a pocket full of them to use as pencils. The burnt end would be enough to write an answer on the paper.

I think my teacher felt sorry for me, and she would send me to the store for her every day at lunch to buy her a candy bar and get one for me. That candy bar every day was the most precious thing in my life at that time.

Not having a pencil motivated me to strive to be better than my classmates. I remember years later when in high school I did most of the teachers' boards that required artwork, and when there was time for a parade I helped on most of the floats.

I'm describing all this to paint a picture of my early life no food, no clothes, no real beds, no TV and no radio. Life in the poverty-stricken, dysfunctional O'Bryant home was always chaotic.

My mom had eleven children before she was thirty years old. One died, and I remember being in the hospital when my mom was in delivery. It was a hard pregnancy and the doctors sent people out to find my dad who showed up drunk and shouting and cursing everyone out. The doctors aid Mr. O' Bryant, you have to decide if you want your wife to live or the baby to live. He replied, F & that bitch, I want my child to live.

All I know is that my mother's life was saved.

Burn the Houses Down

My mom set our houses on fire, sometimes while we were inside. Thinking back, I believe she was sick and tired of the life she found herself caught up in. She had ten children, a drunk and violent husband who beat her almost every day, and often beat the children too.

We moved from one dilapidated shack to another. At one house I remember seeing my mom set rags and paper on fire in a closet, with us still in the house. She walked out and never looked back. We got out safe, and as soon as we did the whole house fell in. I looked down the road to see my mom walking along this country highway as if nothing was going on.

At one house we were so hungry we begged for food from neighbors, mostly poor people like us. They gave us canned food from the government, called commodity. We all had a few cans each, and we played hide and seek outside, running around to find a place to hid our food. Some of us dug holes in the ground and buried the cans to dig up later and eat. Usually the food was cherries or some other fruit. One of my little sisters had some bread that she buried; that night a dog found it and ate it, and I remember how she cried the next morning, jumping up and down saying that dog ate my bread. I felt sorry for her; she must have been thinking how good the bread would be to eat the next day. She was heartbroken.

When I was ten, my siblings and I all went into foster care. Two of my siblings were adopted. I remember the day the white government vans came to our house to load us up. The neighbors had been complaining that my mom and dad were neglectful and alcoholics.

The older children ran to my grandmother's house about a mile away. The rest of us were rounded up; then the vans went to my grandmother's house to get the rest. We were taken to the next down, placed in an apartment and kept under watched by social workers from the Department of Human Service (the Welfare Department) in Mississippi.

They found my mother and brought her to the apartment the next morning. They set her down and told her that they would give her that apartment, a 5-bedroom, and she could put two children in each room. They would pay the bills and give her food stamps to buy food. All they wanted was for her to stay away from her husband and raise her children.

My mother got up, walked out the door and never looked back. The social workers then got busy making phone calls, trying to find families that would take us into foster care. The two youngest children, my little brother and sister, were adopted. I haven't seen them in over 42 years.

The three oldest boys were placed together, the two oldest girls were placed together, and the rest were split up. My family has not reunited since that day. Most of us became alcoholics and addicts.

I spent two years in foster care, in a home with nine other foster kids. I ran away every chance I got. The foster home was in a rural area about ten miles from the nearest town, and I would run and hide in the woods every chance I got. One time I made it all the way to town by following the road and hiding in the woods along the way. I found the welfare office and told them I was not going to stop running away until they sent me back to my momma and daddy.

They did. At the end of that school year I was taken home. My parents took me uptown to be shown off like some price my dad had won.

My hometown is rural, all African-American and small, with a population of between two and three thousand people. I spent one night with my parents and went to school the next day. On the way home, all the kids broke out running toward my mom and dad's house, where I had just spent the night. The house was burning. The house I thought would be next home with my parents. The dream and hope of being a family went up in flames.

A Grandmother's Love

My grandmother was my mom's mom. She was the hardest- working woman I've ever known.

She became my guardian when I was in the sixth grade. Everyone knew I had lost my brothers and sisters so I was considered a social outcast. I started feeling inferior, and alone, and I became a loner.

So my way of coping at school was to study hard and become smarter than the bullies who tried to pick on me and the girls who teased me because I was quiet and shy.

Home life at my grandmother's was confusing. My grandmother still had five children at home, my uncles and unties, and I was older than some of them. I wasn't so well accepted by these uncles and aunts.

My grandmother had three jobs. She cooked at the elementary school, scraped cotton out of cotton fields for a few hours and worked at cleaning a laundromat in the evenings.

When I arrived there, it was summertime and that meant it was cotton-picking time for most of the kids in town. Picking cotton was a way for children to earn money for school clothes and help parents pay bills.

My grandmother did more than just pick cotton. We picked cucumbers, squash, and bell peppers. Fights would break out in the fields among people trying to steal others baskets, and I always had to defend my aunties and my baskets.

This was a way of life for this community. The town was actually a historical town with an interesting history. But the corrupt city government and poor management caused the town to die out.

I started junior high school and my life soon became one of anger and rage.

The Lost Child

Lost can hardly describe the feelings I felt in school I attended after 6th grade.

I found alcohol and marijuana, and I was no longer the quiet shy kid. I had my first spiritual awakening when I had my first drunk.

I started stealing one of my uncles_ beers, and watched where he hid his liquor so I could steal that too. Then I found out that the winos who hung around town would buy me a bottle if I would buy them one. So every night before I would go to bed I would run up town, take about five minutes, pay someone to buy me a bottle and save it for school the next day.

In 8th grade I was selling weed for one of my teachers. I was now the man. I had customers and money and girls and I was popular. By the time I was in the 8th grade I was drinking every day.

My grades started going down, I started staying out later and later and hanging out in the streets. I enjoyed the streets, the clubs, the bars and the crazy world of alcoholics and drug addicts. These were my kind of people and I felt at home with them.

I was done picking cotton. Selling weed and hustling on the pool table was my way of making money.

My mom and dad plus some uncles and family friends were out in this environment, and they would always try to run me home. I refused to go home. I stayed with my grandmother but I had no real home. I would still see my dad uptown, beating up on my mother at night.

My dad did a lot of gambling while drunk and losing all his money on the dice tables so I started hanging out in the gambling rooms to make sure my dad didn't get cheated, but it never worked; he was always so drunk. I would watch him lose hundreds of dollars in the end. At first he would start out winning before the liquor caught up with him. He would drink two to three fifths a night, straight out of the bottle. There were always fights, always pistol plays and always a trip to jail for disturbance of the peace.

I would head home to my grandmother's late at night or early in the morning; someone would get up and let me in.

By the time I was in tenth grade, I was a full-fledged alcoholic. I had to have it and always got someone to buy me a bottle before I went home at night so I could have it in the morning. On lunch break I would run off campus and get someone to go in the liquor store and buy me a bottle. After school I just hung out uptown in the local juke joint, shooting pool and selling weed.

By the time I was in the tenth grade my alcoholism and weed addictions caught up with me. I started stealing and committing burglaries to get money. I eventually ended up in jail as a ward of the state. My grandmother refused to get me out. While I was there, I came to the realization one night, lying on that hard metal bed with those round metal bars, that I had no life, no family and nowhere to go of my own choosing.

I was sent to a house out of town for troubled teens until I was ready to go to Job Corps. This house was a small mansion in a large city with a full staff that fed us, took us to movies, the park and the malls to shop. I didn't even know that such a world existed. I had never been out of my rural, poverty-stricken hometown.

It was good to get away, and I wanted to live in this house forever. The husband and wife who were in charge at the house took a liking to me, and the impression they made on me lasts to this day. They always gave each other compliments, always hugged one another, and said I love you, dear love, with a pure, beautiful smile. I often looked deep into their eyes to see if I could figure out what made them so happy. I wouldn't understand the source of that happiness until many years later.

There were some other kids at the house. Some were older and some were younger than I was but we all had one thing in common the will to survive and the desire for peace from a chaotic world of dysfunctional families.

The day came for me to leave. I was sad. The other kids hugged me and cried. This was a close to a normal family as I had ever had, and I had come to love them.

The houseparent took me to the greyhound bus station. Fred, the husband, had some parting words for me. He said, Johnny, life ain't always going to be what you want but you can be anything you want to be. Just trust in God.

We said goodbye, and I got on the bus. Immediately I felt alone and lost.

On My Own

The bus ride was a big adventure for me. I got a window seat and watched the world go by. I read the signs on the side of the highway, looked at the towns we drove past, and wondered to myself why my life was a mess. Why were my parents alcoholics, and where were my brothers and sisters and what were they doing with themselves?

By now I was smoking cigarettes and still drinking. We arrived at the largest Job Corps site in the nation, with five thousand kids from almost every state. This was a town, like a world of its own. People stuck together by states, and every state had its gang leader and thugs. It was a new world for a country kid from Mississippi. I had to learn to grow up fast, and I did.

We were housed at an old military base dormitory, in with 20 guys downstairs and 20 guys upstairs.

After I'd been there three weeks, a group of guys came in our dorm with sticks and knives, and demanded all of our money. We had just gotten our first allotment of five dollars; they called in the Flying and it flew right out of our hands and into the hands of that gang.

I started school there, got my GED and took up a trade in architectural drafting and carpentry. I was starting to dream of going to college and becoming someone, with an education and a degree in architecture. But it all came to an end around the thanksgiving holidays. We got a monthly allotment of about 50 dollars to buy clothes and toiletries. But the guys in my dorm decided we should all go AWOL. We'd go off campus, buy some beer, liquor, cough syrup and marijuana. Most of us put our money together and six of us went into town through the woods and got the stuff.

We made it back safe about four hours later and got loaded, then paranoid. We barricaded ourselves inside the dorm. The Job Corps police force was called; they shot tear gas through the dorm windows to flush us out. I ran out and right into a staff member who tried to restrain me. I fought back, so ended up with an assault charge and locked up on campus. I was put in a room that had nothing in it, only a hole in the floor, for three days. That hole was my toilet.

Once the three days were up, the authorities gave me two choices: go to court to answer for my behavior, or join the Army. I chose the Army.

Soldier

In the Army, I got through basic training pretty well. I had been on a drill team at Job Corps, so I already knew how to march and make formation. I made squad leader and really enjoyed it. We regularly snuck out of our barracks at night to buy weed.

My grandmother came to my graduation and that

made me feel really good, as though she might have forgiven me for all the wrong I had done.

After basic training at Fort Dix, New Jersey, I went to Fort Gordon, Georgia to train for my MOS (communication specialist). After completing that training I was stationed permanently at Fort Polk, Louisiana. There I discovered a world of addiction like none I'd ever known. The guys at my base had wall lockers full of all kinds of drugs, and I started experimenting with them. I mostly stuck with alcohol and marijuana, and just used more and more. After a while I was a blackout drinker. I started missing work and morning formation, and eventually was discharged with an honorable discharge.

I was glad to be out of the Army, and decided to return to my hometown.

Return to Family

When I got back home, I discovered that I had two younger siblings that had come back from foster care and were being raised by my grandmother. Our older sister had returned, and was well on her way to starting her own family. My older brother was in and out from time to time, and the rest of my siblings were starting families wherever they were. The two youngest siblings had been adopted when our family was separated; those records were sealed and we didn't know where they were.

I had no home to return to. My home was the streets, and that's where I lived. The town had no businesses and no jobs; even if there had been work available, I preferred the street life, the hustle, the chase, and the chaos. I eventually went back to selling drugs and doing whatever I had to do to support my habit. Mainly I stole stuff and sold it, which led to an eventual arrest for burglary and another trip to jail. I stayed in jail for several years.

Life in jail was shocking. I was a loner and I dared anyone to look my way. I carried two homemade knives every day, and went to lock down as punishment every time I got caught with them, but I was determined not to die in jail.

By the time I was released I had had a long time to think and reflect, and had decided that I had learned my lesson and wanted to live a different life.

I got a job working in the construction industry and soon met the young lady who would become my wife.

Marriage

We dated a few times and I moved in with her. We eventually moved from an apartment into a house. She had two young children; we got married within a year and life was pretty good the first few years.

Eventually I started feeling tied down so I started having affairs. I started lying, staying out more and sometimes not coming home at all. My drinking went to another level. I would drink just to deal with life. So we decided to try and see if having a child together would bring us closer, and it did for a while. My wife got pregnant, and it was an extremely difficult pregnancy. There were scary moments when we thought she would not make it.

I wanted this child and cut back on my drinking, trying to be there every day for her.

I remember one time we thought she had had a miscarriage. I prayed to God a lot, in fact, I made a vow to God that went something like this: God, if you would bless us to have this child and comes into the world healthy, I will preach your word for the rest of my life.

My wife had the child, a healthy son, and I forgot I had ever made that vow to God.

The marriage had some good times, but eventually it hit the rocks, mostly due to my drinking and adulterous affairs. After about nine years of this troublesome marriage, my wife said she had had enough. She told me she was leaving to find another to help her raise her kids, and she left.

I thought she was joking; we had broken up and made up many times over the years. But this time she was serious and she didn't come back.

When I finally realized she really wasn't coming back, I felt abandoned. Life as I knew it was over.

Drug Addict

My wife moved out and left me in the house. I became depressed, wasn't working, didn't pay bills and my drinking increased threefold.

I would pass out in my front yard in a blackout, and my neighbor would drag me into the house. I would wake up and not remember. I finally moved out, unable to live in that house without my family.

I went home where my brother and sister lived, and there I was introduced to crack cocaine. Most of my friends were addicts, and I always tried to keep a relationship going with a non-addict so that I would have a place to live. So I ended up in a lot of unhealthy relationships that landed me in and out of jail for petty offense. This went on and off for a year or so.

Finally I was committed to a treatment hospital due to issues relating to my addiction. I spent nine months in treatment there, and was diagnosed with major depression.

After completing treatment there I went back home and decided I needed to relocate. I moved to a larger city and went into a drug rehab program for veterans. That program provided housing and required all participants to become gainfully employed. I went back into construction and was able to start my own construction business, becoming a licensed, bonded, insured contractor. I also teamed up with a couple of Christian friends and started six sober living houses. I wrote the program and was the director of the operation. It lasted about a year, after which my partners wanted to put everyone out and sell the houses for profit.

I had employees living in those houses; some of the guys I hired eventually went on to start their own businesses.

Resentment is the number one offender for an alcoholic, and I had a big resentment at my partners.

I went home and discovered that one of my aunts had passed away. I had been sober (or, rather, dry, which means not drinking but not working a program of recovery) for almost two years, and I figured I could have just one drink before returning to the city from the funeral. But one drink is too many, and it was almost two months before I left town. I depleted two bank accounts during that spree.

I went back into treatment; this in-and-out routine became a vicious cycle for me for the next few years. I'd clean up, and then relapse over and over again.

Chronic Relapser

I went in and out of at least twenty short- and long-term treatment centers, many times going right back to the same one I had just left a few days or a few weeks before.

My addiction got worse. I managed to keep a place to live from time to time, but often had to stay in homeless shelters or the Salvation Army. I started using pain pills, marijuana, cough syrup and cocaine, many times chasing one drug with another. Overdoses were common; I'd end up in the hospital with tubes down my nose sucking blood out of my bleeding stomach. At one point I drowned in my own blood from a ruptured blood vessel in my nose while in the emergency room.

Every time I thought of the family I'd given away, the businesses I had lost due to addiction, I couldn't bear the feelings so I hid from them by drinking and using more. I had lost everything I had, and contemplated suicide a few times. Most of the time when I used all those drugs at one time I was secretly hoping I would just die. I came close a few times but God wasn't finished with me yet.

Sick and Tired

By now my hip was always in severe pain and I needed a total hip replacement. I had gotten out of treatment and relapsed almost immediately; I couldn't wait to get to the service station on the corner and get a beer. That beer led to my last year in addiction, which mostly consisted of me just drinking to pass out, waking up to drink more and passing out again.

The final run lasted four days. I slept in bus stations and on park benches, or in doorways of abandoned buildings. When I woke up that last morning I didn't want to try any more. I lay on the concrete park bench at around 2:30am; mosquitoes buzzed in my ears and bit me. My feet were hurting and I smelled bad since I hadn't bathed in days. I could see tall buildings and city lights shining in the distance.

I rolled my eyes up to the sky, looked at the stars and wondered what had become of me and my life.

I thought about my family and friends that I used to have, the businesses I lost, all the money I had spent on drugs, alcohol and women. Where had I gone wrong?

God, please don't let me wake up, I said as I drifted back to sleep in a state of mental agony and physical pain.

I woke up on and off through the night until daylight broke through the darkness. I didn't want to put my feet on the ground and try to do what I had done the days before. I had had enough. I was whipped, defeated, beaten down, worn out, tired and exhausted. I had been defeated by alcohol and drugs.

I knew that I was going to die if I continued to live like this, and I had to make a decision to either go on as I had to that certain death, or to surrender. I made a decision. I surrendered. And although I didn't realize it at the time, I prayed the alcoholic's prayer: God, please help me.

My feet were sore and hurting and my legs were stiff and didn't want to move but I staggered to a phone booth and called 911. I told the operator that I needed help and if I didn't get any I was going to walk into traffic and end my life. I dropped the receiver and it swung back and forth as I slid down to the floor of the booth and waited. I don't know how long it was but someone woke me up shaking me, asking if I had called an ambulance. I said yeah, and passed out.

I woke up on the stretcher in the ambulance. The EMTs were trying to draw blood and get my name, date of birth and blood pressure while trying to get an IV started. I had had many trips like this to the emergency room but this one was different. This time I knew I didn't have to live like this anymore.

Why do you treat yourself like this? One of them asked. I didn't answer.

I went back into treatment, to a facility where I had been several times before. On my way there I told myself that this time I would do everything the staff suggested I do. I got an AA sponsor, and that person continues to sponsor me to this day.

My First Speaker Meeting

This is the story I told at my first AA speaker meeting.

I have told my story many other times at speaker

meetings since.

Good evening everyone. My name is Johnny O'Bryant, Jr., and I'm an alcoholic. My sobriety date is August 11, 2011. My home group is A Way Out Study Group of Baton Rouge, Louisiana. My sponsor is Mr. Ray R., also from Baton Rouge.

I want to thank you all for inviting me here tonight to share my experience, strength and hope.

I'm 49 years old, the son of Johnny and Helen Jean O'Bryant of Mound Bayou, Mississippi. I have five brothers and sisters.

This is what it was like for me, what happened and what it is like now. I grew up in a small rural town called Mound Bayou. My earliest recollection as a child was of tagging behind my mother in a cotton field as she picked cotton.

My father was a truck and tractor driver. We were raised in wooden shotgun shacks situated way off the highway in the middle of a cotton field.

My parents were chronic alcoholics. My father was very abusive to my mother and to me and my siblings. My father usually beat my mother most every day, and it was just accepted by the community to see my mother with black eyes and busted lips.

Life was pretty rough for us. We rarely ever had food to eat, clothes or shoes to wear. I remember

59

playing outside in the winter barefoot because we had no shoes.

We moved around a lot, from one shack to another. My mother set a couple of houses on fire, once with us still inside. We often had to go from house to house begging for food.

My childhood in school had its ups and downs. We wore hand me down clothes, shoes that were either too big or too small. We didn't have pencils or paper.

We got picked on a lot by other kids and had to fight when we didn't want to.

By the tenth grade I was an alcoholic and a pothead. I was a juvenile delinquent and a ward of the state. I went to Job Corps, got a GED and took up a trade. My drinking and drug use continued and I got in trouble at Job Corps for fighting a staff member. Afterward I went into the military.

In the military my drinking and drug use continued and I eventually ended up getting an Honorable Discharge. I believe that my Sergeant Major who signed my discharge papers knew that I needed those benefits later because I went into treatment a lot in VA hospitals.

After the military I ended up serving time in prison for a burglary charge. After I got out, I got married and my drinking and drug use continued.

I worked in construction, did a lot of mechanical work on neighbors' cars and built wooden lawn furniture for a living. I cheated a lot on my wife. We are no longer married but she is, to this day, the hardest working and most loving and caring woman I know.

My wife had two children at the time we married and we eventually had a son together. We thought having a child would stop my wayward behavior but it didn't.

However we eventually separated and divorced. My drinking got worse. I turned to heavier drugs and wound up in a psychiatric hospital for nine months.

My drug use continued and for the next few years I was on a roller coaster ride of getting sober, cleaning up then relapsing again, that vicious cycle that our literature talks about over and over again.

I coded several times and nearly died twice. In the end I was homeless on the streets, sleeping on park and in doorways of abandoned buildings.

That's basically what it was like. This is what happened and what it's like now. I went into treatment for the last time in 2011and got a sponsor while in treatment. When I got out I found my way to an AA meeting and got another sponsor. I joined a home group that was actively involved in a 12 Step workshop and also did a Big Book study.

I got involved in service work, opening and closing up meetings, making coffee and sponsoring members of this program.

My sponsor got me immediately into taking all 12 Steps. We worked them together. I had a spiritual awakening as a result of working the 12 Steps.

Thanks for allowing me to be here tonight and may God bless and keep us until we meet again as we trudge the road to happy destiny. Good Night.

Father and Son

It is with the greatest sense of love and respect that I write these words about me and my son.

After attending my son's draft party, I headed back to Houston, TX to start my journey of recovery.

Not long after my son and I started talking, mostly by text messages.

He had at least a thousand questions and wanted a thousand answers. He asked me if I would be willing to come to Baton Rouge and Support him on his journey of becoming a great player. The word great caught me off guard. I had never known anyone that wanted to be great.

So I said yes and headed to Baton Rouge. I entered a long-term treatment program to support my recovery and to ensure I had a foundation to build on.

After treatment I moved into a sober living house where my son and I could meet often. My son was there for me. I had apprehension on how I should act and what I should say. I was always saying. Please forgive.

My son told me one day, Pops the past is behind

the both of us. I've forgive you, you're here now and that is all that matters. That statement rocked my world. It made me look at life from a different point of view and also allowed me to move forward without reservations.

We made a pact to have lunch or dinner once a week. I had an opportunity to share my life experiences with him and was not judged or condemned but was only encouraged to do better.

When I did my first art show my son was there to support me. When I did my second art showing he was there to encourage me.

Basketball season after basketball season, I was always there to support him, in his good times and in his low times too. We were there, pushing each other to the next level, to succeed against the odds.

No matter what we faced, we were there, supporting and encouraging one another.

After entering the NBA draft and getting picked up by the Milwaukee Bucks, my son made several trips back here to let me know that he loves me and that I need to continue my journey to become great.

He has said that he understands why I want to be a substance abuse counselor and minister. He has seen me stand behind podiums and share my experience, strength and hope.

My son has been my biggest supporter and pushes me to the limit, to be the best I can be. I can honestly say that my son has shown me how to love unconditionally.

Thank you son for being there for me, and believing that everything I need in life I already have & I just need to use it.

Love you too

Red Stick Louisiana

I ended up in Baton Rouge, Louisiana after going into treatment in a center not far from the city.

My son was in Baton Rouge playing basketball at LSU and working on his dream of becoming a professional basketball player. I was completely caught up in my addiction during his growing-up years and barely ever saw him or supported him and his mom.

But after I left the last treatment center he asked me if I would come to Baton Rouge to support him on his journey. I was shocked by his request, but made it to Baton Rouge to see him.

I barely recognized him. The boy I had barely known had become a 6-foot 9-inches tall college basketball player.

Johnny O'Bryant III, my son, accepted me for who I was and forgave me for what I had done. I made my 9th Step amends to him and we became very close.

In Baton Rouge I moved into a sober living house. He was there for me, picking me up, taking me out to dinner and making sure I was at every LSU basketball home game.

In the last three years we have become the best of friends. I came to love my son, to appreciate him for allowing me to become the father he needed in his life.

My ex-wife came to town often and she was there for me as well. She forgave me and we became friends; they became my biggest supporter. She called a lot, wanting to know how I was doing.

My son has moved on now; he is a professional basketball player in the NBA. I was able to be there at his NBA draft party, clean and sober.

While here my son gave me my one-year and two-year medallions marking years of AA sobriety. He came to speaker meetings where I told my story. He returned to Baton Rouge after being drafted to give me my 3-year medallion.

These were his exact words. Pops you're the greatest man I know with the greatest story I've ever heard. Don't run away from problems. You have told me to face my problems and God will see us through them.

And God has seen me through all my problems. I'm currently in school with plans to graduate as a substance abuse counselor. I'm presently employed in a treatment center as a mental health tech. My plan is to become a Counselor in Training, then a Counselor, facilitating process groups for those who still suffer from the disease of alcoholism.

When I got to Baton Rouge I also joined a church that I now call home. I attend Sunday School and Bible Study on a regular basis and my son has been there for me, sitting beside his pop, supporting me all the way.

I think of the vow I made to God when my wife was pregnant, and we thought we might lose our son, the vow in which I told God that if he would bless us with a healthy child I would preach His word for the rest of my life. The vow I forgot about as soon as my son arrived, healthy.

When my son got drafted into the NBA, that vow to God came back to mind and wouldn't go away.

I prayed to God often for clarity and I realize that I felt called by God to honor that vow. I discussed this with my pastor and he said if I feel I've been called to minister, he would be pleased to work with me. We meet often and go over lessons for growing one's faith in preparation for ministry service. It is my long-term goal to become a Christian counselor.

The burnt matchsticks I used to do my schoolwork because I had no pencils have now become oil pencils and paint brushes. I have actually helped put together a group of artists called Artists in Recovery. There are about fifteen of us, from all walks of life working in all media, and we have had our own art show. I have also mounted my own individual show as part of a local event, with 24 matted and framed pieces. I am working on doing another show, which I hope will be my biggest and best collection, with several different forms of expression and media.

Letting go

The fellowship of Alcoholics Anonymous is most definitely a we program and it took me a while to comprehend the concept that I couldn't do this by myself. I had to depend on those who had found a way out.

I had always had relationship problems and trust issues, especially relationships with males in authority positions. I initially avoided getting a sponsor because I figured a sponsor was someone in authority who wanted to control my life.

I also began to understand that the belief systems I created as a child, to survive, were now harmful to me. I was looking at life through the eyes of a hurt, abandoned, abused, neglected child whose needs were never met. I had become a shame-based person, full of fear, and with low self-esteem.

I had been carrying around hurt that had been handed down to me by my parents who were themselves carrying around hurt that had been handed down to them from their parents. My morals, values and principles were created out of a belief that I would never be anything because my dad ended up being nothing but an abuser and my mother ended up being a chronic alcoholic who had neglected and abused her children.

Early on in life I never really finished anything I started. I remember I couldn't accept a compliment from anyone. I would always work hard to achieve something and right before it would be finished I would find a way to destroy it. I would tell myself that

I didn't deserve it. I always lived in an imaginary glass house that always caved in on me the moment that success was about to happen. I wasn't taught how to create goals and I lost my way in life.

So by the time I crawled into the rooms of Alcoholics Anonymous I was broken spiritually, mentally depressed, physically exhausted and all of my problems in my opinion were the fault of someone else. Usually God.

When I started using alcohol and drugs, I started blaming God for all my problems. If He was God, all-Powerful and all-Knowing, then why did I have to be born to the parents He gave me? Why couldn't I have had parents who weren't alcoholics, who had jobs, a good home, with food and clothes and the ability to raise their children?

Oh no, I had the worst parents and the worst life any child could have had, or so I thought until I came to the program of recovery and heard some of my sponsees' 5th steps.

If it wasn't God that was the problem, then it was the parents, or the teacher, or the sergeant, or the ex-wife, or the boss, or anyone except myself.

Having become a chronic relapser, going in and out of detox and treatment centers, I had a general idea of what I was supposed to do. I was supposed to get a sponsor who had a sponsor who had taken him through the steps to find a God of his understanding so he could have a spiritual awakening. AA terminology for _spiritual awakening is simple it is a personality change sufficient to bring about recovery from alcoholism.

The Student is Ready

I was ready and I knew that the sponsor I chose would not be an African American. I had spent my life running away from African-American males. I didn't want these guys to get close to me and I would find excuses to never be friends with one. I didn't want one for a boss or supervisor or teacher or mentor.

In taking the steps I came to understand that I had developed a flawed and defective belief system that most African-American men were not trustworthy, because that is how I felt about my father. I've since let go of that belief and now have some great friendships
with African-American men.

So the sponsor I chose was an older white gentleman, and now I know that he was the person that God had chosen for me.

I was fresh out of treatment and had made my way to this group called A Way Out Study Group that had been founded by the man I asked to be my sponsor.

This was not an open workshop meeting. The group conducted a 12 Step workshop where newcomers are taken through the 12 Steps in a 4-week period every month except December. The workshop is called Back to Basics.

My sponsor suggested I go through this 12 Step workshop with a Back to Basics sponsor and afterward he and I would meet once a week or so and work the step more thoroughly.

When I got to the meeting place for the first meeting, there were at least seventy people milling around; there was laughter, small talk, catching up. There were people from all walks of life, of all races.

Going inside I saw people making giant pots of coffee and arranging chairs in a certain pattern. Then I saw my sponsor coming toward me. Johnny, he said, can you help these guys get these chairs put out? I said sure. He said he was glad I could make it and he looked forward to working with me. I thanked him.

I was scared to death. Someone was looking forward to working with me. Good luck to him, because he had a job on his hands if he thought he could fix me and help me stop drinking.

The meeting started and the people started coming in. I was surprised to see so many people in one room, all of them supposed to be alcoholics.

In the front was a row of tables with nine people sitting facing the crowd. The Chairperson was in the middle, with four people on either side of her.

Sitting in the chairs along the side walls and along the back were people who had already gone through the steps and were back to sponsor newcomers. That would be me the newcomer.

The meeting opened with the Chairperson explaining the group format. We were given the history of how the group was founded and a brief history of Alcoholics Anonymous.

Week One consisted of the sponsor and sponsee getting to know each other, talking about powerlessness, and going over the first eight pages of Bill's Story so that the newcomer could compare himself/herself to Bill W., one of the founders of AA.

Newcomers would be asked to think about whether they were alcoholics, and were to ask themselves why they couldn't stop or stay stopped, to demonstrate proof of powerlessness. Then it was explained that we would find the Power.

Week Two was designed to help the newcomer find a way to overcome the lack of power, to access the Higher Power by working the action steps (4 through 9). Newcomers learn the 3rd Step prayer, and do the 4th Step inventory using the Back to Basics worksheet. Sponsors help newcomers understand the 5th step, and help make sure that the 4th step inventory is thorough, with no secrets held back. After doing the

5th Step, the newcomer is asked to read the 7th Step prayer, then to go back and read page 64 of the Big Book Resentment is the number one offender._

In Week Three, sponsors and sponsees review steps 6 and 7, pray the 7th step prayer. Then they work on making the 8th step list. In making the amends, the wording to be used is _I was wrong when I _____. What can I do to make it right? For the 9th step amends, it is emphasized that the amends be made wherever possible, not whenever possible.

The meditation process is explained and sponsees are asked to practice meditation before the next meeting and to be prepared to make at least one amend.

Week Four address the amends list and reviews the newcomer's meditation. Then it is suggested that the newcomer find someone to sponsor, or at least come back and help in the meeting.

And basically, that is how I was taken through the steps and asked to come back and sponsor someone the following month. My sponsor told me to be there thirty minutes early to help set up, and I was there every week.

I got on the panel up front and read for over a year, sponsoring guys almost every month and had regular sponsees besides the ones I worked with in Back to Basics.

My sponsor took me everywhere he went. I was on conference committees, and was selected as the group's service representative. I started going to all types of AA business meetings all over Louisiana. I started speaking at different AA meetings, spoke at treatment centers, hospitals and halfway houses.

My life took on a whole new meaning. I eventually got around to working the steps with my regular sponsor, and finished finding out the things that had been separating me from God and the people in the world. I had other groups I attended and did service work in those groups. I got there early and I stayed late after the meetings. I had a host of friends from all walks of life. And finally, after taking the steps, I felt free. I had identified that drinking was just a symptom of my problem. I had to get down to causes and conditions.

So in doing the 5th step with my sponsor I was able to do a personal house cleaning as our literature calls it. I was able to let go of resentments I had been holding on to all my life. I was able to see that the people who had wronged me were perhaps spiritually sick and I was also able to see that I had been spiritually sick and had wronged others.

Step 9 (Made direct amends to such people wherever possible except when to do so would injure them or others, allowed me to make amends and take action to set right the wrong I had done. I learned how to continue to make amends in my daily life.

Step 10 says Continue to take personal inventory and when we were wrong promptly admitted it.

Step 11 says Sought through prayer and meditation to improve our conscious contact with God as we understood him, praying only for knowledge of

His will for us and the power to carry it out. Today prayer and meditation are a part of my daily life.

The whole purpose of taking the steps is to have a spiritual awakening and so to help another sick and suffering alcoholic.

A time to forgive

I recently had an opportunity to go back home where all of this started. I've been afraid that I would never be able to successfully go back without relapsing but I've been back, and have had the chance to visit my parent's graves.

My mom and little brother are buried side by side. Approaching the graves I could feel the memories coming back the good and the bad. After I became an adult, got married, I started visiting my mom's house and we were able to have something of a mother/son relationship before she died.

I read her name on the tombstone, read the inscription, squatted down on top of her grave and just meditated. I felt a sense of a kindred spirit, a sense that she was okay wherever she was. I wanted her to know that I understand her pain of having suffered abuse at the hands of my dad for decades.

Tears gushed out of my eyes and I just cried. I don't know for how long but I just let them flow. I knew that I didn't need to stop them that my soul was healing and also forgiving her but also accepting that by the grace of God I was still here to forgive.

I stepped over a few feet and squatted on top of my little brother's grave. He died such a sad and depressing death. He literally drank himself to death. He was also a diabetic and suffered seizures.

Due to his diabetes, he started having to have toes cut off, then one leg, then the other leg until he was sitting on two stumps. He continued to drink and use drugs until the day he died from complications relating to alcohol.

My dad is not buried at the same graveyard.

His grave is across town in the potter's field. I drove across town wondering what I would say at his grave. There are no tombstones at the potter's field, just a grass field, but I know where his grave is. I went there many years ago when it had a wooden cross on it.

When I made it to the spot where I was sure my father is buried, I sat on the ground and ran my hand through the grass. The city keeps the field cut and clean. I briefly reflected on how mean of a person my dad had been and wondered if he had ever done any good in his life.

People in town loved my dad when he wasn't drinking. He helped everyone out, except that when he drank the worst came out. I silently told him in my heart that I forgive him and that I realize he was an alcoholic who had a disease of addiction. Once he started drinking he couldn't stop; the mental obsession kicked in and then the physical craving and off to the races of another blackout.

I walked away from the grave feeling relieved. The presence of God in me was what helped me to forgive my dad. I had to also make amends for the feeling I had had for my dad and asked him to forgive me for disliking him all my life.

I'm better and feel that finally I've received closure on the world of the past.

Substance Abuse Counselor

I didn't grow up in life saying I wanted to be a Substance Abuse Counselor. I grew up wanting to find a way to die. The emotional pain I carried was too much to bear. Having lost conscious contact with God,

I felt I had nothing to live for so I may as well drink and use until I had a heart attack or stroke. I have had feelings of despair until at times I just wish I could have evaporated off the face of the earth. That way I wouldn't have had to work at becoming an honest, productive member of society.

But that's not how God planned it. It turned out I did want more meaning in my life and when working with sponsees I started noticing that some guys had serious, deep-rooted issues that may require counseling and therapy.

So I enrolled in the Louisiana Association of Substance Abuse Counseling and Training class. I didn't want to take this training online. I wanted to do it in the classroom and I wanted to see if I could commit to finishing this twelve-month training.

My reasoning was that I needed to be sure that this was my calling and my ministry. I wanted to be able to be more than just an AA sponsor. I wanted these people to know that I had been where they were, or had been, and had found a way out only by the grace of God.

Call To Ministry

I must say, as I write these words, that God has a way of bringing the best out of the most horrific events.

Looking over my life, I would have never dreamed that I would one day aspire to become a minister or even a counselor.

I called the pastor of my church one day and told him about the vow I made to God, and that after my son had become a professional basketball player, the memory of that vow came back and God had let me know that he had honored it he had fulfilled his side of the bargain.

I had abandoned my son, and left him to grow up fatherless. But he did not allow that to stop his dreams. I, on the other hand, had become an addict, and eventually a counselor studying with my pastor to become a minister.

I began praying to God for an answer. I believe I received that God is directing me to become a Christian counselor, to fulfill my vow by entering a career in the field of addiction. In this way I believe I can be of maximum service to God and the people in the world.

As I said, God really can and does bring the best out of the worst situations.

Vision of the Church

I arrived at Faith Chapel Church of God not long after my arrival in Baton Rouge. I wanted to be part of a church family and I joined and rededicated my life to serving God all the while working on my recovery while supporting my son as he worked on fulfilling his dream of being a great basketball player.

It came to my attention from going to church that the church had been working on a plan to build a new church across the street and that the members have had this vision for years.

I attended a power point First Peek presentation by the architectural firm hired to design the new place of worship. Sitting in church and hearing the goals and plans that were presented to the congregation, I knew that God wanted to use me. I feel that God has stirred up my heart to help Faith Chapel make their dream come true.

I started praying and asking God how I could be of help and I was given the prayer of Jabez on which to pattern my faith and dependence. After an AA meeting I walked into a small thrift store looking for a new book to read and saw, lying face-up on a shelf, a book titled The Prayer of Jabez. I've always loved that prayer and have read many books and heard of many organizations that have had great success using it in believing in the impossible. So I understood that it is my job to act on faith.

So at session with my pastor I shared that I feel that God wants to use me. I said I don't know how He plans on doing it but I believe and know that it is His will. I have faith that by the time this book is published the ground will have been broken for the new church, and the foundation already laid.

I end this chapter with an appropriate Bible verse: John 16:24 (NIV): Until now you have not asked for anything in my name. Ask and you will receive, and your joy will be complete.

The Family After

My family relationships have not changed much since our family was separated in 1972.

My mother passed away several years ago due to circumstances related to her chronic alcoholism. She died from taking medication that resulted in heart failure.

One of my siblings died at a very early age from alcohol-related illness. I still haven't located my two youngest siblings who were adopted and may have had their names changed. I continue efforts to located them, seeking closure for myself.

I am divorced from my son's mother. Even though I abandoned her, her children and our son, she has been very supportive in my recovery. She continues to encourage me to become the man she believes I can be.

My son has been the biggest influence in my journey during the three years we spent together in Baton Rouge. He attended speaker meetings where I spoke. He has challenged me to become great. We were able to forgive one another and support each other on our own individual journeys.

My son has been one of my greatest teachers although he grew up fatherless. He found me and allowed me to be a father to him. He has encouraged me to keep pushing, to keep going. He has told me that

I'm one of the greatest men he knows, with one of the greatest stories he has ever heard.

My friends and associates in recovery have allowed me to put my hands in theirs and we are trudging the road of recovery together. Today I have a host of friends from all walks of life: doctors, lawyers, engineers, pastors, nurses, counselors, teachers and other friends, all living clean and sober.

Getting to where I am today has been some of the hardest work I've ever had to do. It has required total dependence on God. There were times when I wanted to give up.

My worst point in recovery came when I was unemployed, lost my health insurance and my car insurance, my bills either doubled or tripled, my phone was disconnected and I didn't want to accept it.

I prayed and prayed, and God directed me to let go of it all and to trust in Him. That was the hardest decision I have had to make. I had to lose it all to build my faith and see the power of God at work. Things got better gradually.

God is everything or He is nothing. What is the choice to be?

Life has gotten busy. I try to maintain that perfect balance, but in my current line of work, I hear one sad story after another. I've seen sponsees die, and had friends and friends of friends die from alcohol and drug-related problems.

I'm grateful to the fellowship of Alcoholics Anonymous; it has helped me recreate my life.

There's a church to be built and that's where you'll find me, working for God to help expand His kingdom here on earth.

Or you'll find me at the treatment center where I work as a mental health tech, waiting on my certification as a Counselor in Training. I plan to continue my education.

When I get a break, you'll find me with a paintbrush in my hand, creating a new piece of art.

It's a long way from the shack in the cotton field in the Mississippi Delta, wearing a flour sack and picking up matchsticks to write with at school.

The sky is the limit and I'm only limited by my refusal to become teachable.

Johnny O'Bryant, Jr. and Faith Chapel

There are four persons who are currently responding to the call of ministry at Faith Chapel. Brother Johnny O'Bryant, Jr. started coming to Faith Chapel when he was living in a group recovery home within walking distance of the church. Johnny is a committed member of the Faith Chapel congregation currently for at least two years. While continuing to be involved in his personal ministries and supporting his son who was then attending LSU, Johnny has become a faithful servant of God, attending Bible study and regular worship. Lately he has entered into in a one-on-one discipleship mentoring program with the senior pastor. Johnny has informed the senior pastor that from his younger years the Lord had a specific call on Johnny's life for the preaching ministry. The senior pastor has a firm belief that it is his responsibility to help persons under his parish care to fulfill and develop their ministry calling to their maximum expression. The mentoring program in which Johnny is now involved has a comprehensive focus on spiritual formation, ministry gift development and quality of personal life, family and social life. The senior pastor explains that it is a joy having Johnny as a member of Faith Chapel's fellowship, and a joy working with him toward his calling in Christ Jesus.

Faith Chapel's Building Ministry

Recently Johnny has expressed his deep desire to see a much-needed new building for Faith Chapel come to fruiting. Faith Chapel's senior pastor, elders and building committee members presented a schematic design in October 2014 for a new, comprehensive sanctuary. Due to the growing ministry needs in four key areas - worship, administration, fellowship and discipleship the Faith Chapel congregation made a decision to build a new building to accommodate the current status of ministry and give room to grow One of the greatest outstanding needs for more space has to do with children's and youth ministry. Faith Chapel regularly picks up about seventy children and youth each Sunday, feeds them breakfast, has Bible study for Sunday school and then children's church for ages 4_10 during the regular worship hour. Just ministering to seventy children alone has created a good but real problem of space needs.

There are needs for adequate classroom space (possibly up to nine class rooms) to cover all children and youth ages as well as at least two adult classes, young adults and middle age to senior adults. The building project, which will seat about 325 persons in both the worship area and fellowship hall along with adequate bathroom space, classrooms and administration, will cost about $2.5 million.

The senior pastor was greatly encouraged by a recent visit from Johnny, as Johnny spoke words of affirmation that he believed that the Lord was going to help Faith Chapel, its leaders and members to build this much-needed facility. The Faith Chapel congregation looks forward to occupying its new building hopefully by the end of 2016.

A History of Faith Chapel Church of God

In August of 1948, Reverend George W. Burns, an African-American pastor in New Orleans, Louisiana, received a letter from Sister Rose Williams about the need for a colored church in Baton Rouge. In response to that letter, prayer meetings were started at Sister Pearl Davis_ home on Staring Lane with a group that accompanied Rev. Burns from New Orleans. A Sunday School was also started and an acre of land was donated by Sister Davis_ husband. The Evangelistic Committee of the white assembly, along with College

Hill Church of God and the black assembly, pooled funds and began work on the first church building in 1949. Brother Burns, Brother Tackett, Brother Charles Wilson and others came to assist with the building.

The new group's first trustees were Sister Rose Williams, Brother George W. Burns and Sister Leteff.

Brother Charles I. Wilson III was the first pastor and served from 1949 to 1952. Brother Wilson recruited children and brought them to church in his truck, including children from Blundon Home, who continued to be part of Faith Chapel's ministry until the mid-sixties. Reverend Olita Fontenot was the interim pastor for a brief period. Rev. Rose and Brother Bill Williams pastored for fifteen years. Rev. Rose Williams was a white woman who was harassed by the Ku Klux

Klan and the White Citizen's Council as she worked with blacks, but God's protection around her and the congregation continued to grow. When the church outgrew its first facilities, plans were made for a larger building. With a $12,000 loan from the Board of Church Extension and Home Missions in Anderson, Indiana, the new facility was erected in 1968.

Sisters Rosella Williams and Wilhelmina Haney were interim pastors for three years after Reverend Rose Williams suffered an accident which prevented her from serving further as the pastor. In 1974, Brother J.D. Brown became the pastor. Three years later in 1977, the mortgage was paid off for the sanctuary and in 1983 the Educational Building was erected.

The ministries of Faith Chapel include a dynamic Vacation Bible School, Children's Program on Saturdays, and a prison ministry (including ministering to prisoners_ families and to ex-convicts), Sunday School and ministering to the aged. During Pastor J.D. Brown's thirty-five years of pastorship, Faith Chapel flourished. Five ministers were ordained (Deidra Johnson, Lynette Fontenot, Rica Kwentual, Barbara Williams and Eric Johnson) and Pastor Brown encouraged, supported and mentored the development of a number of young preachers, including Ryan Fontenot and Adam Kwentua. He coordinated the prison ministry for nearly thirty years and mentored others to continue the work upon his passing. Pastor

Brown partnered with Pastor Azouro to establish the Christ the King congregation in Baton Rouge, a largely African congregation.

Lastly, Pastor Brown encouraged the congregational support of the South African mission project at Kokona Dikgale Primary School that continues to this day.

Reverend Rosella Williams served as Assistant Pastor throughout Pastor Brown's tenure. After Pastor J.D. Brown died in August 2007, Reverends Eric and Deidra Johnson served as interim leaders of Faith Chapel. In November 2008, Reverend Eric Johnson was elected Senior Pastor of Faith Chapel and he served in that capacity until April 5, 2010. On July 11, 2010, Faith Chapel appointed Reverend Barbara Williams as interim pastor until June 30, 2011. Then on July 1, 2011 Pastor Bartholomew Riggins was elected as Faith Chapel senior pastor. Pastor Riggins is the present senior pastor for Faith Chapel Church of God.

Ecology of Ministry at Faith Chapel

Faith Chapel serves its members and the surrounding communities through many ministries. Our motto of Extending and Equipping in Excellence is at the center of each ministry's mission On the other hand, each ministry also serves to reach persons based on either gender or age-related missions. All of the ministries Men's Fellowship, Christian Women's Connection, Youth Ministry, Sunday School, Children's Church and Saturday Program as well as the Usher. Board and Prayer Ministry, are promoted by leaders and individuals who have a heart for Jesus and a desire to see those in their target group disciple, involved and equipped in God's Word. Along with discipleship, our ministries are also the vehicle we use, in addition to Sunday Worship Services, to grow the church and perform many types of community outreach. Service is at the heart of all ministry efforts. For many years

Faith Chapel has operated a bus service that picks up children and adults in the South Baton Rouge area. We are also the lead church in the Gardere Initiative, a consortium of churches that serves the needs of underprivileged children and adults in the Gardere area. Another service we offer is tutoring (LEAP testing) for fourth and eighth grade students. We also offer yearly scholarships to members who are enrolled full-time in college. Electronic media is another area of outreach that we employ.

Our website, www.faithcahpelbr.com, is in the process of becoming fully developed and is highly trafficked by our members and others wanting to get to know us better.

Faith Chapel Church of God is a Bible-based non-denominational church that is family-oriented, Christ-centered, member-supported, mission-minded and involved in the community. We are also formally with Church of God Ministries, Anderson, IN. Historically, Faith Chapel followed a ministry structure of two main governing bodies - a Board of Trustees and a Church Council. In 2006, Pastor J.D. Brown led the congregation in converting to an elder board structure which eliminated the need for trustees and a church council.

FCCHOG is a full-time congregation in the greater Baton Rouge, Louisiana area in a urban setting, predominantly African American. Faith Chapel has five ordained ministers, one licensed minister and four persons who are in their early stages of response to the call of ministry. FCCHOG, a full-time ministry with office hours Tuesday through Friday and Sundays, has an intentional focus for both internal and external ministries having recently opened up an apartment home for ministry intervention in the Gardere area of East Baton Rouge Parish.

Keith Gillespie, _History of Faith Chapel,_ (paper presented for forty-fifth annual Louisiana General Ministerial Assembly campground celebration, Baton Rouge, LA, May 2010).

Graduate Day

Its three thirty a.m. in the morning I awake from a restless sleep and immediately my thoughts goes to the graduation. I've successfully completed the counseling training. A year long course through the Louisiana Association of Substance Abuse Counselors

and Trainers. The Dire ctor has asked me if I would be willing to do the Invocation Prayer and I agree. I start composing a draft and worked on it for almost three weeks to get it down to a science. I'm pleased with the finished product. I've read it so many times I almost have it memorized.

I toss and turn as I think of the day ahead. It has been a lot of fun going back to school, learning about Pharmacology, Counseling Theories. Counseling

Process and Counseling Techniques. All at the same time interacting with the other students. We've discussed some controversial topics and had some heated discussions but overall it has been very educational. My approach has been to stay open-minded. I've learned that there is no one way or approach to treating a person. There are so many different methods, theories, opinions, suggestion, techniques, diagnosis, medications and treatments it's a lot to comprehend.

My approach has been more of a holistic spiritual educational and religious view of treatment. So I believe in God, Jesus Christ, Medicine science and the 12 Steps of recovery. In essence my goal is to eventually become a Christian Counselor. The digital clock now says it is four thirty seven a.m. I may as well get up. Class starts at 8:00 and by the time I get ready, do my morning meditation and have breakfast, read my morning devotional books eight a.m. will not be far off.

What to wear? This is our biggest graduation class this year. There are twelve of us. There is a graduation every quarter, so with twelve of us graduation, plus family and friends coming we are looking for a large turnout. What to wear is contingent on the size of the crowd. I always try to look my best no matter what, today is extra special. I rummage through the closet and go with a gray suit. I'm a little nervous, I've never graduated before much less successfully completing an educational training program. This is progress for me. I bathe, afterwards I pray and meditate then I read my two meditation books. I always end with a short passage out of the Bible.

As I'm getting dressed I recite the Invocation Prayer out loud. I arrive to class early and have breakfast in the facility cafeteria alone. I can see a few classmates passing by thru the glass window in the door. This is our last class and we'll graduate later in the day. I'm a little defocused due to my anxiety of having to recite the Invocation Prayer. Class lets out a little early and some of us volunteer to get the room ready. Soon after the family starts arriving, along with friends and guests.

We open with the introduction by the Director. I'm called to recite the Invocation Prayer. I recite intuit goes well. We're called one by one to receive our diploma and take a picture with the Director. Next we're all asked to come forward and share our experience of why we want to be a Substance Abuse Counselor. We take individual and group pictures. The day finally ends and I'm pleased to officially receive my diploma as a Counselor in training.

Currently I'm seeking employment as a Counselor in Training. My main focus centers on my Ministry studies working toward becoming ordained and combining Ministry with counseling to become a Christian.Counselor. Ultimately my long term goal and vision is to become a National Motivational speaker by sharing all my life experience.

Never Ever Give Up.

Play It Forward

Good bye to Mom and Dad

As I grew up watching my parents bizarre behaviors and dysfunctional lifestyles as a little boy it at first seemed normal and because it was situational and environmental I just wanted to get out of the confusion. When I was eighteen years old my mom stabbed my dad in the chest with a steak knife in the house they lived in together. He dies immediately. I never really got the truth of what took place that day. I heard many stories and scenarios. If I had to say for sure what happened, my mom was tired of being physically and emotionally abused and finally stood up for herself.

The price she would pay is that it haunted her all the rest of her life. At first it was bad, she drown her pain with alcohol. The law said it was self- defense so she was cleared of all charges. My Dad was around 40 years old when he died.

After becoming an adult and returning home and starting a family myself I knew I had to go to my Mom and face her and tell her that I forgive her for everything that happen. My Mom's death was another situation that I really never go clarity on. I was in treatment when she died and didn't make it to the funeral. I was told by family members that she died from complications due to her drinking and taking medications. That she had a heart attack while standing she fell and hit the side of her head on the corner of an end table and died from a head injury.

My Mom and Dad has passed on and as I shared in and earlier chapter I said my goodbyes at their graves after all these years. I receive closure in a dream with my Dad. In a dream I was with about thirty children around the age on ten. We were all playing and we were surrounded by angels and above us white doves flying very softly and gently. It looked like we were in another dimension of existence. There were no walls or floors as if we were suspended in space that we did not need gravity to hold us in place. My Dad magically appeared and walked between the children and came directly toward me holding a bundle of large purple grapes stretched out his hands and offered me the grapes. As he did he looked into my eyes and I looked up and into his eyes and asked me, point blank, son will you please forgive me?_ I simply said yes and the angels around us started moving, the dove started flying faster and the children started laughing and

127

clapping. My Dad vanished in all the activity and I woke up wondering what had just happen. I conclude that God made it possible for me to forgive my Dad.

As time passed the anger and bitterness I felt toward my Dad vanished. I am finally free from all the pain and suffering I experience as a hurt, abandoned, emotionally, physically abused child. It is over, finished, done. I can't change the past. I don't know what the future holds all I know is all I have in life is one breath at a time that is given to me by God that turns into minutes, hours, days and years. This very moment is all any of us have. Thank God for it. Who knows when the last one will be taken.

My promise to God

I never dreamed or thought that one day I'd be writing a book and telling the readers that I promised God that I will work diligently to help a church be built and that my goal is to help raise funds toward that vision, from the proceeds of this book. This has only been discussed in private with the Pastor and now it is time to proclaim it to the world. Earlier I spoke about the Prayer of Jabez in in believing in something so big that it will take an act of providence to be fulfilled. I know it will take the power of God to bring this into existence. I wait on God as I work. My close friends and some associates often tell me that I am crazy to try and raise such a large amount on my own. One case in particular one of my dearest friends has said man you are almost homeless, you have no money, you won't ever be rich or famous, you're just wasting your time trying to help build a church. Get a minimum wage job or two of them and just try to make it. Stop living in a fantasy land.

There are the non-believers who have said take out the section about the church it has nothing to do with your story. I kind of laugh to myself because my faith is in God and God does not fail, neither will Faith Chapel. This is the second publication of this book, again I was

told, man just give it up and don't worry about it, you aren't going to make it. At first it was my son who encouraged me, I've surrounded myself with men of God who believe in me and believe in God and believe in a new church.

Dearest Readers, I would like to say thank you for your interest in my story. God had other plans and the message is simple by the loving grace and mercy of God my acceptance of Jesus Christ as my Lord and Savior.

I've committed my life to serving Jesus and doing what the word of God says. Mark 16:15 and he said to them,

Go into all the world and preach the gospel to all creation New American Standard Bible.

Closing Remarks

I'm appreciative and thankful to God for giving me strength, courage and determination to change. All my life I ran from adversities, my failures use to define me but today I use my failures as an opportunity to build my character, maintain integrity, grow more dependent on God and believe in myself. Is it easy? Of course not, it requires a complete physic change in my mental attitude, the willingness to become completely humble and sacrifice one_s life to serve Jesus Christ and God, that the reward and the price to be paid.

My new found journey is a road less traveled and as I venture into this unexplored territory of living life as a Counselor in Training, Minister in Training, Self-Published Author and Artist, these accomplishments and achievements is only shaping me into the man God wants me to become. So suffering must be embraced as something great, a condition and situation in life imposed by God that has helped me to work toward fulfilling my fullest potential as a human being. Using the talents and gifts God has given me to grow spiritually, mentally, emotionally and physically to be well and whole.

He who can conquer himself can also conquer a city by himself. All my success and achievements if that is what they are called is due solely to trusting in God and my faith in our Lord and Savior, Jesus Christ.

Things That Have Been Helpful

Believing in the Power of God
Church
Bible Study
Counseling Training
12-Step Program
Sponsorship
Working in Treatment Center
Mentorship
Ministry Studies
Forgiveness
Acceptance
Making Amends
Prayer
Meditation
Volunteering
Therapy
Believing in Myself
Believing in Others
Helping Others
Holy Bible
The Big Book of Alcoholics Anonymous
Twelve Steps and Twelve Traditions Book of Alcoholics
Anonymous
Meditation Book
Speaking at AA Speaker Meetings

Conclusion

We would love to hear from you at Faith Chapel Church of God.

Address:

Faith Chapel Church of God
995 Staring Lane
Baton Rouge, LA 70810

Administration Assistance: Karen Williams

Email: karenwilliamsfccog@aol.com

Phone: 225-766-4512

Fax: 225-766-4512

Website: www.Faithchapelbr.com

Pastor: Rev. Dr. Bartholomew M. Riggins, Senior Pastor

We ask for your continuous prayers as we believe
God will bless us in our vision to build a new church.

From Rags to Riches
Spiritual Riches Order Form

Orders: www.fibersoflife.org

Postal orders: P.O. Box 80222, Baton Rouge, LA 70898

Telephone orders: 225-955-6089

Email: frtsr2015@gmail.com

Book Price $14.95

Shipping: $3.99 for the first book $1.50 for each

additional book.

Coming soon to Amazon, Barnesandnoble .com

Format: print, eBook and notebook

For booking, speaking engagements, and interviews

contact Johnny O_Bryant, Jr. @ 225-955-6089